Tips for Reading Together

Children learn best when reading is fun.

- Talk about the title and the pictures on the cover.
- Discuss what you think the story might be about.
- Read the story together, inviting your child to read with you.
- Give lots of praise as your child reads with you, and help them when necessary.
- Try different ways of helping if they get stuck on a word. For example: read the first sound or syllable of the word, read the whole sentence, or refer to the picture. Focus on the meaning.
- Have fun finding the hidden space bugs.
- Re-read the story later, encouraging your child to read as much of it as they can.

Children enjoy re-reading stories and this helps to build their confidence.

Have fun!

Find these 10 space bugs hidden in the pictures.

The Spaceship

Roderick Hunt • Alex Brychta

OXFORD

UNIVERSITY PRESS

Floppy went to sleep and
he began to dream.

A spaceship landed.

"Wow!" said Kipper.

"A real spaceship!"

An alien came out.

"I am Zig," he said.

"And this is my dog, Zog."

"Let's go into space," said Zig.

"Oh yes!" said Kipper.

"Oh no!" said Floppy.

WHOOSH! The spaceship
took off. It flew up into space.

"What's that?" said Kipper.

"Oh no!" said Zig. "Fireballs!"

WHOOSH! Suddenly, there
were fireballs all around them.

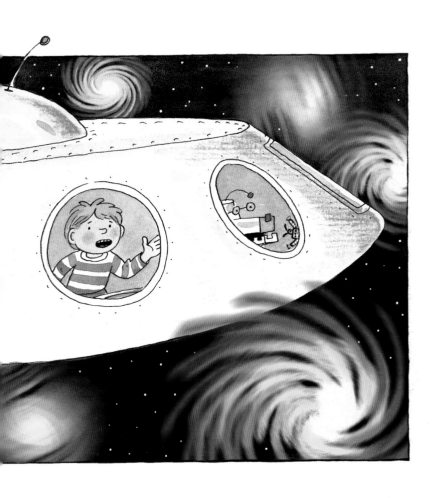

"Help!" said Zog.

CRASH! A fireball hit them.
The spaceship began to
spin round.

Zig and Kipper bumped heads.

"Oh my head!" said Kipper.

"Oh my head!" said Zig.

Floppy saw a very big fireball.
It was going to hit them!

"Help!" said Floppy.

"We're in danger!" said Zog.

"I don't know what to do."

"I know what to do," said Floppy.
"I can fly the spaceship."

ZOOM! Floppy flew the
spaceship out of danger.
"Phew! Just in time," he said.

"Well done, Space Dog Floppy,"
said Zig. "You saved us!"

Think about the story

Why did Floppy dream about space?

How did Floppy feel about being in space?

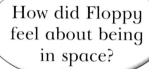

Why did Floppy have to take control of the spaceship? How did he know what to do?

Where do spaceships go in space? Where would you like to go?

A Maze

Help the spaceship find its way through the fireballs
to the Earth.

More books for you to enjoy

Level 1: Getting Ready

Level 2: Starting to Read

Level 3: Becoming a Reader

Level 4: Building Confidence

Level 5: Reading with Confidence

OXFORD
UNIVERSITY PRESS

Great Clarendon Street,
Oxford OX2 6DP

Text © Cynthia Rider 2005
Illustrations © Alex Brychta 2005
Designed by Andy Wilson

First published 2005
All rights reserved

Series Editors: Kate Ruttle,
Annemarie Young

British Library Cataloguing
in Publication Data available

ISBN 978-019-279244-0

10 9 8 7 6

Printed in China by Imago